WORLDWIDE SUPERSTARS

Richard J. Brenner

EAST END PUBLISHING, LTD.
Miller Place, New York

This book is dedicated in loving memory to my mother, Betty Brenner, who taught me to judge people by their character, and not by the color of their skin, their country of origin, or their system of belief. And it is also dedicated, as all my books are, to the children of the world. I wish that each of you could live in peaceful surroundings; free from fear and bigotry of every type, and I hope that you will always stride, with courage and compassion, toward your sweetest dreams.

I also want to express sincere thanks to Ed Masessa, Janet Speakman, Roy Wandelmaier, Lori Grafstein, and Alan Boyko for their continued support, as well as to Alfred Mercado, John Douglas, Elliot Markham, and Bob Christopher.

Book Design: **Alfred Mercado**   Copy Editor: **John Douglas**

Photo Credits: The image of Ichiro Suzuki on the cover and the one on P. 46 was photographed by **Otto Greule, Jr.** and supplied by Getty Images. Icon SMI supplied all of the remaining images. The cover image of Albert Pujols and the one on P. 5 was photographed by **Ed Wolfstein**; P. 6 by **Peter Newcomb**. The cover image of Johan Santana and P. 20, **Duncan Williams**; P. 8, **Anthony J. Causi**; P. 9 **Rhona Wise**; P. 11 **Rich Kane**; P. 12, **Anthony J. Causi**; P. 14 & P. 15, **John Cordes**; P. 17 N/A; P. 18, **Christophe Elise**; P. 21, **Anthony J. Causi**; P. 23 & P. 24, **John Cordes**; P. 26, **Bob Levy**; P. 27, **Christophe Elise**; P. 29, **Chris Williams**; P. 31, **Ed Wolfstein**; P. 32, **Bob Levy**; P. 34, **Edmund J. Szalajeski**; P. 35, **Christophe Elise**; P. 37 & P. 38, **Matt Brown**; P. 40 & P. 41, **Brian Jenkins**; P. 43, **Scott D. Weaver**; P. 44, **Rhona Wise**; P. 47, **Christophe Elise.**

ISBN: 0-943403-76-6 * 978-0-943403-76-2

Published by EAST END PUBLISHING, LTD.
18 Harbor Beach Road
Miller Place, NY 11764

Printed in the United States of America by R.R. Donnelley

Richard J. Brenner, America's best-selling sportswriter, has written more than 80 exciting sports titles. For details on how to order some of them, see the back of this book.

*   *   *

Mr. Brenner is also available to speak at schools and other venues. For details, including fees, you may e-mail him directly at: rjbrenner1@gmail.com, or write to him c/o EEP, 18 Harbor Beach Road, Miller Place, NY 11764.

AUTHOR'S MESSAGE: For many years, Native American groups have been appealing to sports teams not to use names and logos that many people find offensive. Out of respect for, and in support of those appeals, I have chosen not to use such names in this book.

This book was not authorized by Major League Baseball or by any of the players in this book.

INTRODUCTION

Although baseball was tagged as the *national pastime* of the United States in the middle of the 19th century, the major leagues didn't field a team west of or south of St. Louis until 1957, when the Brooklyn Dodgers moved to Los Angeles and the New York Giants migrated to San Francisco. In addition to being geographically challenged, major league baseball couldn't be considered national in another sense, since black people weren't allowed to play on any of their teams until 1947, when Jackie Robinson was recruited to break the color barrier and to begin his Hall of Fame career with the Dodgers.

Latino players, who also had to overcome the prejudice that was endemic in baseball, started to break into the majors in significant numbers during the 1950s and 1960s, when such future Hall of Famers as the Venezuelan-born Chicago White Sox shortstop, Luis Aparicio, and Roberto Clemente, the Puerto Rican-born right fielder of the Pittsburgh Pirates, paved the way. Today, Latinos represent a sizable percentage of the rosters of big leagues teams and many of them are among the game's brightest stars, including Albert Pujols, Johan Santana, and Adrian Gonzalez.

The influx of Asian players, which only began in 1995, when Hideo Nomo, a right-handed pitcher from Japan, signed with the Dodgers, has already produced a number of top players, including Ichiro Suzuki, Daisuke Matsuzaka, and Chien-Ming Wang.

Just as the sport wasn't truly national for a great many decades, it wasn't in any way global, despite calling its championship the World Series. In fact, every major league franchise was located within the borders of the U.S until 1969, when the Montreal Expos joined the National League. Since the Expos moved to Washington D.C. in 2005 and changed their name to the Nationals, the Toronto Blue Jays, who joined the American League in 1977, remain the only franchise that is currently located outside the U.S.

Despite that history of geographic exclusion, the major leagues have, in recent times, tried to reach out and truly globalize the game, most notably by championing an international tournament, the World Baseball Classic, which brings together teams from 16 countries.

The initial WBC championship, which was played in 2006, was won by the Japanese squad, which defeated the entry from Cuba in the finals. Three years later, in the second staging of the WBC, the Japanese team triumphed again, by beating the team from South Korea in the championship round. Ichiro drove in the game-winning runs against the Korean team, while Daisuke Matsuzaka, who picked up three wins in each of the two tournaments, was named the MVP for the second successive time. Although the WBC is imperfect in many ways, including issues of scheduling and player participation, it is a sincere attempt to bring people together and to give the sport a truly global presence.

Author's note: The individual statistics cited in the rectangular stat boxes, which appear on the first photo page for each player, don't represent either a single-season worth of numbers, or cumulative career averages, but rather uses each player's career statistics to extrapolate what numbers a player would achieve in a 162-game schedule.

Richard J. Brenner

ALBERT PUJOLS
ST. LOUIS CARDINALS

First Baseman

Born: January 16, 1980, in Santo Domingo, Dominican Republic
Height: 6-3   **Weight:** 210   **Bats:** Right   **Throws:** Right
Round Drafted: Thirteenth (1999)   **Major League Debut:** April 2, 2001

Although the question is not beyond debate, most baseball professionals and outside experts consider Albert Pujols to be not only the best player in the game today, but one of the greatest ever to grace the diamond.

"Right now, he's the top all-around player in baseball," said Hall of Fame manager Sparky Anderson. "Before he's done, we might be saying that he's the best of them all."

Pujols, who emigrated to the United States from the Dominican Republic when he was 16 years old, burst into the big leagues by setting National League rookie records with 130 RBI, 88 extra-base hits, and 360 total bases. The St. Louis Cardinals' slugger also cracked 37 home runs, posted a .329 batting average, and was a unanimous choice as the 2001 NL Rookie of the Year.

"For Albert to do what he did for six months is just phenomenal," said Cardinals' manager Tony La Russa. "If he had been a 10-year veteran, it still would have been exceptional, but to have done it in his rookie season is just unbelievable. Everything about Albert is legitimate, and he's going to be doing this for a long time."

Although rookie accomplishments are certainly no guarantee of future success, with many Rookie of the Year Award-winners fading into mediocrity or even total obscurity, Pujols has gone on to prove that his manager's words were right on the mark.

During his eight complete seasons in the majors, Pujols, with a pair of MVP trophies, a Gold Glove, and a batting title, has played to a level that is unique in the history of the game. He is the only player ever to start his career with eight straight seasons with a .300 batting average, and at least 99 runs, 30 home runs, and 100 RBI. He has also reached 300 career home runs faster than any other player and his .335 career batting average and .626 slugging percentage rank first among all active players.

"He is the whole package," said La Russa. "He commits to defense just like he does to offense, and he is one of the best base-runners around. I always tell young players that if they want to learn how to do things the right way, they should just watch Albert."

As far as La Russa is concerned, however, what sets Pujols apart has as much to do with his work ethic and his intense dedication as it does with his talent. Pujols is constantly working on all aspects of his game, spending as much time on fielding drills as he does in the batting cage.

"He is the classic complete player, and it's not just about his physical tools," said La Russa. "I've never seen a player who has a better understanding of the game, or a greater desire to win. Everybody has an ego and everybody wants to put up good numbers, but Albert has always put winning way above his pursuit of personal goals."

"I won't say flat-out that he's the greatest player of all-time," added La Russa. "But, what I will say is that you can't have a conversation about the subject without putting him into the mix."

ALBERT PUJOLS

HITS	HR	RUNS	RBI	BB	SB	OBP	SLG	AVG
200	42	124	128	93	7	.427	.626	.335

CARLOS BELTRAN
NEW YORK METS

Center Fielder
Born: April 24, 1977, in Manati, Puerto Rico
Height: 6-1 **Weight:** 190 **Bats:** Switch-hitter **Throws:** Right
Round Drafted: Second (1995) **Major League Debut:** Sept. 14, 1998

Carlos Beltran, who was born and raised in Puerto Rico, first caught the eye of baseball fans in 1999, when he was named the American League Rookie of the Year. The switch-hitting center fielder had shown a world of promise during that initial season by racking up 27 homers, 108 RBI, and 27 stolen bases for the Kansas City Royals.

"With his physical attributes, he has the potential to be an All-Star year in and year out," declared Allard Baird, who was the Royals' general manager. "What's scary is that he still hasn't put it all together."

Beltran moved further into the national spotlight in 2004, after a June trade had sent him to the Houston Astros. His insertion into the lineup had jump-started their offense and helped them surge into the playoffs. Then, he proceeded to put on the most dazzling display of postseason hitting in baseball history.

Beltran began the fireworks when he bashed four big flies and set a National League division series record by driving in nine runs against Atlanta. Two of the homers and five of the RBI came in the decisive, win-or-go-home Game 5. He continued his astonishing work with the stick against the St. Louis Cardinals in the National League Championship Series by stroking four more dingers and scoring an LCS-record 12 runs in the seven-game series. The eight home runs that Beltran tallied in only 12 games, tied the single postseason record that had been set by Barry Bonds over the course of 17 games in 2002.

"He was hitting balls off his shoe tops for home runs," said former big league outfielder Cliff Floyd. "It was unbelievable. You couldn't turn off your TV. You had to watch him."

After the postseason had ended, Beltran signed a free agent contract with the New York Mets, who expected him to become the centerpiece of their team in 2005. Those expectations were disappointed, however, because Beltran, who was slowed by a leg injury and who also felt uncomfortable in a locker room full of strangers, turned in a sub-par season.

"I felt alone," explained Beltran. "When I was having difficult moments, I didn't have a person that I felt comfortable going to talk to about it."

The Mets altered the dynamics of the team in 2006, primarily by trading for first baseman Carlos Delgado, who provided another veteran presence on a team that had been filled, mostly, with younger players. Beltran responded to the changed atmosphere by racking up career highs in runs scored, home runs and RBI in 2006, and he has continued to be a powerful presence in the middle of the Mets' lineup ever since. He's also fulfilled the prediction made by his former general manager by being named to three successive All-Star teams, while also winning a pair of Silver Slugger Awards and three Gold Glove Awards.

"He's such a dominant player," said Mets' manager Jerry Manuel. "He can take over a game in so many different ways."

CARLOS BELTRAN

	HITS	HR	RUNS	RBI	BB	SB	OBP	SLG	AVG
	177	29	113	108	76	30	.360	.483	.283

MARIANO RIVERA
NEW YORK YANKEES

Pitcher
Born: November 29, 1969, in Panama City, Panama.
Height: 6-2　　　**Weight:** 175　　　**Bats:** Right　　　**Throws:** Right
Round Drafted: N/A　　　　　　　**Major League Debut:** May 23, 1995

Although Mariano Rivera has been widely judged to be the best closer in baseball history, when the New York Yankees signed the pole-thin Panamanian in the winter of 1990, they couldn't decide which pitching role he was best suited for. During his first six seasons with the organization, Rivera was actually used more as a starter than as a reliever. It wasn't until 1996, his first full season in the majors, that the Yankees' brass finally decided to use him exclusively out of the bullpen.

"Mo would have been successful at any position they put him in," said Yankees' shortstop Derek Jeter. "I came up with Mo when he was a starter, and no one hit him then. It was pretty impressive."

During the 1996 season, Rivera served as a setup man for John Wetteland, a pill-throwing closer who led the American League in saves, and who then went on to capture the MVP trophy for his extraordinary efforts in the World Series. But, the Yankees had so much faith in Rivera's ability to assume the closer role in 1997 that they didn't re-sign Wetteland.

"John had been great for us," said former Yankees' manager Joe Torre. "But we felt that Mo was ready for the job."

Despite that vote of confidence from his manager, Rivera blew three save opportunities in the first month of the 1997 season, and the shaky start undermined his sense of self-assurance for a while. But, with the help of his own inner toughness and the encouragement of Torre and Mel Stottlemyre, who was the team's pitching coach, Rivera settled in and closed out the regular season by converting 43 of his 52 save opportunities.

"I realized that as long as I did my best, I would be able to sleep at night," recalled Rivera. "A short memory is required in this job."

His toughness was tested again in the postseason, after he failed to convert a close-out opportunity in the first round, and the lost opportunity played a large part in the team's elimination from the playoffs. But, he rebounded big-time the following year, when he plowed through the postseason without yielding a run, and also saved three of the Yankees' four wins in the World Series. Rivera continued his remarkable mastery in 1999, when he was named the World Series MVP and, again, in 2000, when, for the third time in succession, he saved three of the team's four World Series wins.

"If we don't have Mariano, we don't win four World Series," said Yankees' catcher Jorge Posada. "It's as simple as that."

Rivera has continued to post astonishing numbers throughout his storied career, both in the post season, where he owns the lowest-ever career ERA, 0.77, and in the regular season, where he sits in second place on the all-time saves list with more than 500.

"Mo has done things that nobody else in the history of the game has done," said Jeter. "Whenever he's come in, it's been pretty much automatic."

MARIANO RIVERA

IP	HITS	HR	SO	BB	W	L	ERA
81	63	4	74	19	4	38	2.29

JUSTIN MORNEAU
MINNESOTA TWINS

First Baseman
Born: May 15 1981, in New Westminster, BC, Canada
Height: 6-4   **Weight:** 235   **Bats:** Left   **Throws:** Right
Round Drafted: Third (1999)   **Major League Debut:** June 10, 2003

Although Justin Morneau, like any good Canadian, played hockey as a child, he didn't have the talent to play the sport at an elite level. But when it came to baseball, Morneau excelled at an early age, making it seem as though success could almost be taken for granted.

As a high school student he was a member of two National Championship baseball teams, and he was named the tournament's top hitter in 1998. The following year the Minnesota Twins selected him in the third round of the draft, and four years later he was called up to the big club.

Minnesota manager Ron Gardenhire inserted him into the clean-up spot, and Morneau responded by collecting five hits in his first two games for the Twins.

"It's been a lot of fun, but I know that I'm not going to get three hits every game," said Morneau. "I guess there's no way for me to go now but down."

Although he had spoken that last sentence half in jest, Morneau did go into a terrible tailspin at the plate, and was sent back to the minors the following month.

"I started to swing at pitches out of my zone," explained Morneau, who had never before had to take a backward step on the diamond. "Then, I lost my focus and my confidence."

The Twins recalled him in the middle of the 2004 season, and he provided the pop that helped to carry them to a division title by drilling 19 homers and driving in 58 runs in only 74 games. But his production nosedived in 2005, and when the slump persisted into the first 10 weeks of the 2006 campaign, it seemed as though his career was at a crossroads. Some of his teammates were questioning his dedication, and Gardenhire told him that he was running out of patience.

"That meeting with Gardy was a wakeup call," acknowledged Morneau, who immediately began to log extra time in the batting cage. The added work began to pay spectacular dividends, as he went on to rack up 34 homers and drive in 130 runs, which not only helped spark the Twins to a division title, but which also earned Morneau the American League MVP Award.

"It was like a maturity button went off," said Twins right fielder Michael Cuddyer. "I definitely give him a great deal of credit because I know it took a lot of work and a lot of looking in the mirror for him to get to this point."

While Morneau no longer takes his success for granted, he has continued to be one of the top run producers in the American League, averaging more than 123 RBI for each of the past three seasons.

"I've learned that there aren't any shortcuts," said Morneau, who was the runner-up for the 2008 MVP award. "The only way to achieve results and help your team win is to put in the time before the game ever starts."

JUSTIN MORNEAU

	HITS	HR	RUNS	RBI	BB	SB	OBP	SLG	AVG
	169	30	89	117	62	1	.352	.507	.285

HANLEY RAMIREZ
FLORIDA MARLINS

Shortstop

Born: December 23, 1983, in Samana, Dominican Republic
Height: 6-3   **Weight:** 195   **Bats:** Right   **Throws:** Right
Round Drafted: N/A   **Major League Debut:** Sept. 20, 2005

When baseball executives were polled recently about which player they would choose to build a franchise around, Hanley Ramirez emerged as the pick of the litter. When a group of players was asked the same question, Ramirez also topped their wish list.

"He can steal bases, he can hit for power and average, and he plays shortstop, one of the most important positions," said Miguel Tejada, the perennial All-Star shortstop of the Houston Astros. "He can do everything."

Ramirez, who was born and raised in the Dominican Republic, has been a batting star ever since he won a home run contest when he was four years old. But for Ramirez, the sheer joy of playing the game has always meant more than records or even monetary rewards.

"I always loved to play baseball," declared Ramirez. "It had nothing to do with money. I never thought about being a millionaire. I just wanted to play baseball."

The Boston Red Sox signed Ramirez in 2000, and the following year, at the age of 17, he hit over .400 while playing for their entry in the Dominican Summer League. The following year the Red Sox started him off with their lowest minor league team, but he played so well that he was bumped up two levels during that first season. By the end of the 2005 season, Ramirez was rated as the tenth-best overall prospect in the minor leagues by Baseball America and, for the second successive year, the No.1 prospect in the Red Sox organization.

"It's not as though you needed special skills to predict a great future for Hanley," noted Theo Epstein, Boston's general manager. "A fourth-grader could watch him play a few games and see that he's our best big league prospect."

Ramirez had such a *can't-miss* tag on him, in fact, that Epstein was able to trade him to the Florida Marlins for a pair of All-Stars, Josh Beckett, a flame-throwing starting pitcher, and Mike Lowell, a hard-hitting, Gold Glove-winning third baseman.

Ramirez quickly justified the deal for the Marlins by hitting for a .292 average, while swiping 51 bases and smashing 17 home runs, the most homers by a rookie shortstop since Hall of Famer Ernie Banks hit 19 in 1954.

"I don't want last season to be as good as I get," said Ramirez, who was named the 2006 National League Rookie of the Year. "Anybody can have one great year. I have to go out and prove that I can do it year after year."

Ramirez has, in fact, gotten better in each of his seasons with the Marlins, and in 2008 he became only the fourth shortstop ever to steal 30 bases and crack 30 homers in the same season.

"He's the total package, and he's putting it all together at a such a young age," said Chone Figgins, the third baseman for the Los Angeles Angels. "He creates runs and he saves them. He gives his team speed, power, batting average and defense. He's got everything you look for in a franchise player."

HANLEY RAMIREZ

	HITS	HR	RUNS	RBI	BB	SB	OBP	SLG	AVG
	200	28	127	73	70	46	.382	.532	.311

JOHAN SANTANA
NEW YORK METS

Pitcher
Born: June 13, 1979, in Tovar, Venezuela.
Height: 6-0   **Weight:** 195   **Bats:** Left   **Throws:** Left
Round Drafted: N/A   **Major League Debut:** April 3, 2000

During his first three seasons with the Minnesota Twins, Johan Santana spent most of his time in the bullpen, patiently developing his pitches and learning his trade. By 2003, however, Santana, who was born and raised in a small Venezuela town, thought that he was ready to become a full-time starter—an opinion that wasn't shared by Minnesota's management.

"I was upset, but I've learned that even though I can't control situations, I can't allow situations to control me," said Santana. "I was determined to show them that they were making a big mistake by keeping me out of the starting rotation."

Santana finally received the opportunity he had been seeking in the middle of the 2003 season and, after losing his first two starts, he reeled off eight straight victories to end the season.

"When I'm playing video games and I'm the Minnesota Twins, I start Santana and then I bring in Joe Nathan to close out the game," said Los Angeles Angels' center fielder Torii Hunter, who was Santana's teammate in Minnesota. "Santana gets hit in the video games. But, that's only because the games haven't caught up to the reality."

The southpaw got off to a shaky start in 2004 due to off-season surgery on his pitching elbow, and he struggled into the All-Star Game break with a 7-6 mark. But, once he was able to put the fear of cutting loose out of his mind, he closed out the season with 13 straight wins, and became the first Venezuelan-born player to win a Cy Young Award.

Two years later, Santana won his second Cy Young Award, and he made a case for being one of the best pitchers in baseball by leading the league in wins, strikeouts and ERA. It was the first time that a pitcher had captured the Triple Crown since 1985, when Dwight Gooden had turned the trick while pitching for the New York Mets.

"He brings his heat and then he dances his changeup at them, and hitters just can't make that type of adjustment," said Hunter. "He doesn't just make them miss, he embarrasses them."

When financial considerations forced the Twins to put Santana on the trading block after the 2007 season, the Mets were delighted to swoop in and take him off their hands. He quickly started to repay their confidence in him by leading the National League in ERA, games started, and innings pitched.

"He seems to have an innate sense of what to throw and when to throw it that doesn't just come from a scouting report," observed 324-game-winner and Hall of Famer Don Sutton. "He's as polished as anybody pitching today."

Since 2004, in fact, Santana leads all starting pitchers in victories, ERA, strikeouts, and innings pitched, but he's looking ahead to an even brighter future.

"I'm just reaching my prime," said Santana, who can still recall the time when people doubted his abilities. "I have a chance to do something special. I still have a long way to go."

JOHAN SANTANA

	IP	HITS	HR	SO	BB	W	L	ERA
	213	175	23	221	59	15	7	3.06

Right Fielder

Born: February 9, 1975, in Nizao Bani, Dominican Republic
Height: 6-3   **Weight:** 235   **Bats:** Right   **Throws:** Right
Round Drafted: N/A   **Major League Debut:** Sept.19, 1996

Vladimir Guerrero is carving out a career that is, undoubtedly, leading him to the Hall of Fame, but when he does get inducted into the museum, he may rank as the most unselective hitter ever to be enshrined in Cooperstown.

"Man, his strike zone is from his toes to his nose," noted Atlanta pitcher Tom Hudson. "But he hits everything you throw at him."

Guerrero signed with the Montreal Expos, the forerunners to the Washington Nationals, in 1993, when he was 16 years old. The following year, the Dominican-born-and-raised Guerrero was assigned to the Expos' Rookie League team and immediately began his rapid rise to the major leagues. During his three-year apprenticeship in their farm system he scorched minor league pitching for a .345 average, and by 1997 he was the Expos' Opening Day right fielder.

Although an injury limited him to only 90 games in his rookie season, he did hit over .300, a feat that he's accomplished in each of his professional seasons. In his second season, Guerrero set six team records and finished among the big league leaders in 10 major offensive categories. He also joined Hall of Famers Joe DiMaggio and Mel Ott as only the third player under the age of 23 to amass 200 hits, belt 30 homers, and rack up 100 RBI in a single season.

"He's just one of those special hitters," said Atlanta manager Bobby Cox. "I'll bet he's had that same swing since he was six years old."

In his six full seasons north of the border, Guerrero shattered nearly all of the Expos' career and single-season hitting records. During that span he posted a .332 batting average, the third-highest among National League hitters, while his 222 home runs and 661 RBI were the fourth-highest totals in the Senior Circuit.

Following the 2003 season, Guerrero signed a long-term deal with the Los Angeles Angels and immediately impressed his new skipper with his dedication to his craft and his passion for the game.

"He's incredible," raved Mike Scioscia. "From the first day of spring training he was practicing as if it was the seventh game of the World Series."

Guerrero made an immediate impact in the Junior Circuit by totaling 10 home runs and 23 RBI in the final two weeks of the 2004 season, which powered the Angels to a western division title, and earned him the American League MVP Award.

He has continued to be one of the most productive, if unorthodox, hitters in baseball and, in 2008 he became, after the great Lou Gehrig, only the second player ever to hit for at least a .300 average and crack 25 or more homers for 11 consecutive seasons.

"You just can't compare Vladdy to the current crop of players, because he compares favorably to the most incredible players who have ever played the game," declared Scioscia. "You have to chart him against the all-time greats, the Hall of Famers."

VLADIMIR GUERRERO

	HITS	HR	RUNS	RBI	BB	SB	OBP	SLG	AVG
	197	36	104	117	62	16	.388	.573	.322

ADRIAN GONZALEZ
SAN DIEGO PADRES

First Baseman
Born: May 8, 1982, in San Diego, United States
Height: 6-2   **Weight:** 225   **Bats:** Left   **Throws:** Left
Round Drafted: First (2000)   **Major League Debut:** April 18, 2004

Adrian Gonzalez first experienced the joy of playing ball on the streets of Tijuana, Mexico and then in San Diego, California, when the family moved back across the border to the city of his birth.

"We'd just go out and play all the time," recalled Edgar Gonzalez, who is four years older than Adrian. "We had lots of friends and we were always outside playing with them. We played all the sports. Basketball. Stickball. Soccer. Football. We had a really great childhood."

Edgar also remembered how his younger brother had demonstrated the determination that would, eventually, lead him to the big leagues.

"One day Adrian made an error when he was playing in a T-ball game," recalled Edgar. "He came back home and threw a tennis ball against the wall maybe 100 times or more, just because he had missed that one catch. He's always been hardworking, responsible and competitive."

Gonzalez displayed that same drive when it came to his schoolwork by always taking care of his responsibilities before he went out to play.

"Adrian would come home from school and the first thing he would do is his homework," noted Edgar. "He did that as a young kid, and all on his own, without anyone telling him to."

Gonzalez also showed his independent attitude when he quit the football team at East Lake High School because the coach tried to turn him inside out.

"He wanted me to yell at guys, to jump in the huddle and pump guys up," recalled Gonzalez, who was the quarterback for the junior varsity team, and was ticketed to move up to the varsity the following year. "But I told him, 'That's not who I am, so I'm going to play baseball.'"

Football's loss was baseball's gain, as Gonzalez went on to post a .559 batting average during his final two seasons for the Titans, which convinced the Florida Marlins to take him with the first overall selection in the 2000 amateur draft.

While climbing up the minor league ladder, Gonzales was traded first to the Texas Rangers, in 2003, and three years later to the San Diego Padres. During his first three seasons with his hometown team Gonzalez has blossomed into one of the top players in baseball, becoming both a feared slugger and, in 2008, an All-Star and a Gold Glove first baseman.

"He doesn't get the attention that he deserves," noted Troy Tulowitzki, the Colorado Rockies' shortstop, "but he's one of the best players in the league."

But nothing gave Gonzalez a bigger thrill than when he finally got to play with Edgar when the Padres promoted his older brother to the big leagues in May 2008, and then, again, when the two shared the infield for Team Mexico in the 2009 World Baseball Classic.

"It's an excitement that you can only dream about," said Adrian, with the glee that recalled their childhood games. "But now that we are living it, it sends thrills through my body."

ADRIAN GONZALEZ

HITS	HR	RUNS	RBI	BB	SB	OBP	SLG	AVG
172	30	94	98	63	0	.351	.498	.283

CARLOS ZAMBRANO
CHICAGO CUBS

Pitcher
Born: June 1, 1981, in Puerto Cabello, Venezuela.
Height: 6-5 **Weight:** 255 **Bats:** Switch-Hitter **Throws:** Right
Round Drafted: N/A **Major League Debut:** Aug. 20, 2001

Carlos Zambrano is a perfect example of the old adage that says that one shouldn't judge a book by looking at its cover. Although the Chicago Cubs hurler has the physique of an over-stuffed teddy bear, he's not only one of the top pitchers in the National League, but so good with the stick that he's sometimes used as a pinch-hitter.

"People have to realize that Carlos is a ballplayer, an athlete, not just a pitcher," noted Dusty Baker, who managed the Cubs from 2003-2006.

Zambrano began to develop his athletic talent while growing up in Venezuela, although he turned to baseball only after he realized that he didn't have enough talent to become a top-notch soccer player.

"I loved to play soccer," said Zambrano, who can sometimes still be seen kicking a ball around the Cubs' locker room. "But baseball was my mealticket."

Zambrano cashed his first paycheck from the Cubs in 1997, when he was only 16 years old, and it didn't take too long for them to realize that they had a pitcher with a special arm.

"At 19, when he was in the Midwest League, he was throwing 95 mph *in the ninth inning*," recalled Cubbies general manager Jim Hendry. "That showed me that he had a big league arm."

Zambrano received his call up to the Windy City in 2001, and two years later he joined the starting rotation and contributed a 13-win season and a 3.11 ERA. He's been a model of consistency on the mound ever since, as evidenced by the fact that he is the only pitcher in the National League to win at least 13 games each year since 2003.

In addition to his consistency, Zambrano has also shown the ability to be spectacular, as he was on September 14, 2008, when he pitched a no-hitter against the Houston Astros.

"That was pretty exciting," said Cubs' manager Lou Piniella. "He had that great fastball from the first pitch all the way to the end, mixed in some sliders, split-fingers, and beat a team that's really been hot. Just a great game by Carlos."

Zambrano, who had come close to pitching a no-hitter a few times earlier in his career, was ecstatic about his performance and the fact that it had helped the Cubs inch closer to a division title.

"All my pitches were working great today, and when I saw the radar gun clocking me at 98, 99 in the first inning, I thought, 'Let's get it on,'" said Zambrano, who became the first Cub in 36 years to toss a no-hitter. "But, I still can't believe I did it."

Zambrano, who has been a three-time All-Star for his pitching prowess, has also won a pair of Silver Slugger Awards for his hitting, and is the career-leader for home runs by an active pitcher.

"He's a great athlete and a tremendous hitter," said Cubs' first baseman Derrek Lee. "You don't see many guys his size who are that athletic."

CARLOS ZAMBRANO

IP	HITS	HR	SO	BB	W	L	ERA
213	179	18	181	95	15	9	3.51

CARLOS LEE
HOUSTON ASTROS

Left Fielder
Born: June 30, 1976, in Aguadulce, Panama
Height: 6-2   **Weight:** 235   **Bats:** Right   **Throws:** Right
Round Drafted: N/A   **Major League Debut:** May 7, 1999

Carlos Noriel Lee, Jr. learned about life and baseball by tagging along behind his father, who was a star outfielder for an amateur team in Aguadulce, Panama, the small city in which Lee was born and raised.

"He taught me the lessons about responsibility and work ethic that I'll teach my son," said Lee, who served as the batboy for his father's team. "I want my son to learn to work and to know that nothing is given to you. Everything must be earned."

While the experiences he had were rewarding for Lee, they were also a source of great pleasure for his father.

"I was excited when I took him to the diamond," said the senior Lee, who earned his living as a manager at a communications company. "If he had a glove on, he was at ease. He showed interest right away. If you show interest and dedication, you'll get what you want."

Although a scout from the Chicago White Sox signed the teenaged Lee in 1994, his trip through their minor league system was gradual, rather than meteoric. But when he did get the call up to the Windy City in May 1999, he broke in with a bang by blasting a home run in his first big league plate appearance.

"I remember that at-bat," said Lee, whose nickname is *El Caballo*, which is Spanish for *The Horse*. "I was facing Tom Candiotti, the knuckleballer. After he had two strikes on me I told myself, 'Just don't strike out.' And then I was lucky enough to connect. It was a thrill I'll never forget."

Lee quickly established himself as a reliable hitter and run producer during his six seasons with the ChiSox. But despite wielding a big bat, he found himself in the doghouse of Sox' manager, Ozzie Guillen, and after the 2004 season Lee was traded to the Milwaukee Brewers.

Undaunted by playing in a new league, Lee became the leading man for the Brew Crew, collecting 32 dingers and 114 RBI during the 2005 season.

"He never gets panicked or seems to feel pressure," noted Brewers' manager Ed Yost. "He's one of those special players who wants to be '*The Guy*.'"

Unfortunately for the Brewers, they couldn't agree on a contract extension with Lee, so they dealt him to the Texas Rangers on the eve of the 2006 trading deadline. Despite that midseason change of teams and leagues, Lee went on to hit for a .300 average and total 116 RBI and a career-high 37 homers.

Lee, who had become a free agent after the 2006 season, did agree to a long-term contract with the Houston Astros, and he has rewarded the team's huge financial commitment by becoming one of baseball's best and most consistent batsmen.

"He's worked hard to get where he is," noted Lee's father, who closely follows his son's progress. "After Rod Carew, Carlos is the best hitter Panama has ever produced, and my son still has a lot of seasons to play."

CARLOS LEE

HITS	HR	RUNS	RBI	BB	SB	OBP	SLG	AVG
179	31	95	109	50	12	.344	.505	.291

MANNY RAMIREZ
LOS ANGELES DODGERS

Left Fielder
Born: May 30, 1972, in Santo Domingo, Dominican Republic
Height: 6-0   **Weight:** 200   **Bats:** Right   **Throws:** Right
Round Drafted: First (1991)   **Major League Debut:** Sept. 12, 1993

When the 13-year-old Manny Ramirez showed up for his first practice at Manhattan's George Washington High School, the newly arrived immigrant from the Dominican Republic didn't make a great impression on Steve Mandl.

"At first, he was just slightly better than an average player, but he turned himself into a superstar by working harder than everyone else," recalled Mandl, the Trojans' longtime baseball coach. "Before school started, he would lift weights and then run up a hill, dragging a tire behind him. After practice was over—and we practiced from two in the afternoon until 7:30—Manny would keep at it. He was the hardest worker and the best player I've ever coached."

Cleveland selected Ramirez with the 13th overall pick of the 1991 draft, and two years later he was named the Minor League Player of the Year by *Baseball America* after he had hit .333, poled 31 homers and driven in 115 runs in 129 games. That performance earned Ramirez a late-season call-up by Cleveland, which he celebrated by banging a pair of dingers at Yankee Stadium in only his second game on the major league stage.

"He has the sweetest swing I've ever seen," said Charlie Manuel, who was Cleveland's hitting coach. "He's always balanced, and he always keeps his bat level through the zone. I never messed with Manny's swing. By the time he got here, it was already perfect."

Ramirez began to emerge as a big league superstar in 1995, when he won the first of his nine Silver Slugger awards, and he has gone on to become one of the most devastating hitters in baseball history. He reached his apex with Cleveland four years later, when he collected 165 RBI—the first time in 51 years that an American League player had driven in more than 160 runs in a season.

After he'd hit for a career-high .351 average the following year, Ramirez signed with the Boston Red Sox, and began blasting balls off of and over the Green Monster in Fenway Park with amazing regularity. He had a great run during his seven-and-a-half seasons in Beantown, winning a batting championship in 2002, and a home run title in 2004, when he led the BoSox to their first World Series win in 86 years. But the relationship between the team and the player went south during the 2008 season, and he wound up being traded to the Los Angeles Dodgers on July 31.

Ramirez, who ranks among the all-time leaders in all major hitting categories, went on an astonishing tear as soon as he joined the Dodgers, compiling a .396 batting average, and collecting 17 homers and 53 RBI during the final two months of the season. His hitting and his leadership with his young teammates were the engines that drove the Dodgers' late-season surge that propelled them to the NL West Division title.

"He plays in a different league than the rest of us, a higher league," observed Dodgers' third baseman Casey Blake. "He led and we followed."

MANNY RAMIREZ

	HITS	HR	RUNS	RBI	BB	SB	OBP	SLG	AVG
	184	41	111	133	94	3	.412	.594	.315

DAISUKE MATSUZAKA

IP	HITS	HR	SO	BB	W	L	ERA
204	180	22	193	96	18	9	3.92

JASON BAY
BOSTON RED SOX

Left Fielder
Born: September 20, 1978, Trail, BC, Canada
Height: 6-2   **Weight:** 200   **Bats:** Right   **Throws:** Right
Round Drafted: Twenty-second(2000)   **Major League Debut:** May 23, 2000

Jason Bay began his staggered path to the big leagues in the Canadian town of Trail, BC, which sits across the border from Spokane, Washington. His fledgling career actually got off to an auspicious start when he helped his Little League team capture the Canadian championship and earn a trip to the 1990 Little League World Series, where they won one game before being eliminated by a team from Taiwan.

Because his high school didn't field a baseball team, Bay played on an American Legion team in Idaho, but his production there didn't merit a college scholarship offer, let alone a draft-day call from a major league team. Lacking a clear-cut alternative, he decided to play at a small junior college, but he did so well in his two seasons there that he was able to obtain a scholarship from Gonzaga University.

Bay turned in two superlative seasons with the Bulldogs, twice earning all-conference honors, while claiming the West Coast Conference batting title with a .388 mark as a senior. Those accomplishments failed, however, to overwhelm major league scouts, and he lasted until the 22nd round of the 2000 draft, when the Montreal Expos (who have since become the Washington Nationals) finally selected him.

Although Bay won the 2001 Midwest League batting title in only his second season in the Expos' organization, he was traded away the following spring. That was the start of a baseball version of hot potato, which would see the young outfielder traded to three different organizations before he landed on the plate of the Pittsburgh Pirates near the end of the 2003 season.

Bay made a notable impact with the Bucs when he clouted a pair of homers and collected eight RBI in a single contest, and he finished the season by reaching base in 14 straight games. He continued to show that he belonged in the big leagues the following year by banging out 26 dingers and driving in 82 runs in only 120 games, and he was rewarded by being named the first-ever Canadian-born player to win Rookie of the Year honors.

"I never expected things to go this well this fast," said Bay, who also became the first Pirates' player ever to win the award. "I'm just glad that I was able to have a good year and prove that I could play."

Bay added further proof the following year when he made his first All-Star appearance and was the only player in the majors to compile a .300 average and at least 20 stolen bases, 30 homers, and 40 doubles, while topping the century mark in runs and RBI.

Two years later, however, Bay was dealt again, swapped to the Boston Red Sox, as part of a three-team trade that sent Manny Ramirez from Beantown to the Los Angeles Dodgers. Bay quickly endeared himself to Red Sox Nation by helping to lead Boston to the American League Championship Series, while becoming the biggest bat in their lineup.

"We thought we were getting a really good player," said Boston manager Terry Francona. "We just didn't realize how good he is."

JASON BAY

	HITS	HR	RUNS	RBI	BB	SB	OBP	SLG	AVG
	165	32	101	107	86	11	.377	.523	.283

MIGUEL CABRERA
DETROIT TIGERS

First Baseman
Born: April 18 1983, in Maracay, Venezuela
Height: 6-4   **Weight:** 240   **Bats:** Right   **Throws:** Right
Round Drafted: N/A   **Major League Debut:** June 20, 2003

Miguel Cabrera, who was born and raised in Maracay, Venezuela, developed a love for the game by tagging along behind his father, who was a very good amateur player, and his mother, who was the shortstop on the Venezuelan national softball team for 14 years. And he showed so much potential by the time he was 16 years old that the Marlins, who were in a bidding war for his services with a number of other teams, wound up paying him nearly $2 million to sign his first contract.

"He was a natural hitter from the first time I saw him, even at 16, 17," declared Marlins' executive Tony Perez, who was inducted into Cooperstown in 2000 after hitting 379 home runs in his playing days. "He knows what he has to do, and he's always making adjustments to counter whatever opposing pitchers throw at him. Just watch how still he is in the batter's box, and how smooth and compact his swing is. He's as good as it gets."

Four years later, Cabrera stepped on to the big league stage by whacking a walk-off home run in his first game with the Marlins, becoming the youngest player ever to hit a game-winning big fly in his major league debut. Cabrera continued his heroics in the postseason by banging four home runs and helping the surprising Marlins capture the 2003 World Series.

During his five seasons with Florida, Cabrera kept getting better and better, putting up numbers that placed him among the greatest players in the history of the game. He was an All-Star in each of his final four seasons with the Fish, and became the sixth-youngest player ever to hit 100 home runs, and, at 24 years old, the third-youngest, after Hall of Famers Ted Williams and Mel Ott, to compile four straight 100-RBI seasons.

Unfortunately for the always-cash-strapped Marlins, financial constraints forced them into trading Cabrera and pitcher Dontrelle Willis to the Detroit Tigers prior to the start of the 2008 season. Although the Tigers had to surrender six of their top prospects to complete the deal, Detroit manager Jim Leyland declared that what they had received far outweighed the price that they had paid.

"We don't think 24-year-old superstars come along very often," said Leyland. "Sure, we gave up a lot, but you're supposed to give up a lot to get a superstar. You can wait a lifetime to get a player like Miguel."

Cabrera quickly showed that the change of leagues hadn't cramped his style by racking up career-highs in homers, with a league-leading 37, and RBI, with 127.

"Last year I had a lot of adjustments to make in coming to a new league and facing new pitchers, but now, I know what I'm doing," said Cabrera early in 2009, speaking words designed to give American League pitchers a collective nightmare.

"He has the talent and power to be one of the best ever," said Leyland. "If he keeps going the way he is, he'll end up in Cooperstown."

MIGUEL CABRERA

HITS	HR	RUNS	RBI	BB	SB	OBP	SLG	AVG
190	32	99	120	70	3	.384	.543	.312

ICHIRO SUZUKI
SEATTLE MARINERS

Right Fielder
Born: October 22, 1973, in Kasugai, Japan
Height: 5-9   **Weight:** 160   **Bats:** Left   **Throws:** Right
Round Drafted: N/A   **Major League Debut:** April 2, 2001

Ichiro Suzuki was a baseball superstar in Japan before he ever set foot in the United States or played his first game for the Seattle Mariners. Ichiro, who prefers to be addressed by his first name, began his professional career in 1991, at age 18, when the Orix Blue Wave, who play in Japan's Pacific Coast League drafted him. After he had served a two-year apprenticeship in their minor league system, Ichiro was promoted to the major league team and immediately began carving out his legendary career.

In 1994, his first season with the Blue Wave, Ichiro was named the PCL's MVP after he set a single-season record with 210 hits, in only 130 games, and led the league in hitting with a .385 batting average, while also earning a Gold Glove for his fielding excellence.

"I cannot be the player I am without defense and speed," said Ichiro. "I may impress people with my hitting, because that's what most people concentrate on. But it's my defense and running that make me the player that I am."

That was the first of seven consecutive batting titles and Gold Gloves for Ichiro, who also went on to win two more MVP awards, and to lead the Blue Wave to a pair of pennants and a Japan Series title in 1996. After establishing an unrivaled level of accomplishment in Japan, he decided that he wanted to test himself against the competition in the American major leagues.

"It was time to move up," announced Ichiro, when he signed to play for the Mariners in November 2000. "As an athlete, you have to compete against the world's best."

Although many people doubted Ichiro's ability to become the first non-pitcher from Japan to make the transition, Bobby Valentine, who had managed in both countries, was doubt-free.

"He's going to be the Rookie of the Year," declared Valentine. "He's a great hitter, in any league; he runs like a deer, and he has one of the best arms I've ever seen. He's one of the top five players in the world."

Ichiro validated Valentine's prediction by hitting .350 and stealing 56 bases, while becoming the first player since Jackie Robinson, in 1949, to lead the majors in both categories. Ichiro, who was named the American League Rookie of the Year and its MVP, set a number of records in his initial season in Seattle, including most hits by a first-year player, 242, and he also helped lead the Mariners to a record-tying 116 wins.

"He's the engine of our train," said Mike Cameron, who was Ichiro's teammate. "He's the one who makes us go."

Ichiro, who won a second batting title in 2004, when he set the single-season record for hits, with 262, has continued to be the catalyst for Seattle. And, after eight consecutive seasons of earning Gold Gloves and All-Star status, he has also continued to display the same level of mastery in America as he had in Japan.

"This game is just different for this man," noted Paul Molitor, who collected 3,319 hits in his Hall of Fame career. "He sees spaces on the field and guides the ball to where he wants it to go, just as if he was playing slow-pitch softball."

ICHIRO SUZUKI

HITS	HR	RUNS	RBI	BB	SB	OBP	SLG	AVG
229	10	111	59	48	40	.377	.432	.331

ORDER FORM

WORLDWIDE BASEBALL SUPERSTARS:
15 of baseball's best players—including Albert Pujols,
Johan Santana, and Ichiro Suzuki—are profiled in a book
that includes 29 pages of photographs.
48 pages, 8 x 10. $5.99 U.S.

QTY

_____

ALEX RODRIGUEZ * ALBERT PUJOLS: A dual-biography of baseball's
two top superstars. This book includes 16 action-packed color photos.
144 pages, 5 x 8. $5.99 U.S.

_____

TONY ROMO * BEN ROETHLISBERGER: A dual-biography of two football
superstars. The book includes 16 pages of action-packed color photographs.
144 pages, 5 x 8. $5.99 U.S.

_____

TOM BRADY * LADAINIAN TOMLINSON: A dual-biography of two of the
NFL's top players. The book includes 16 action-packed color photos.
144 pages, 5 x 8. $5.99 U.S.

_____

BRETT FAVRE: An easy-to-read photo-filled biography of one of football's
all-time greats. Written especially for younger children.
32 pages, 8 x 8. $4.50 U.S.

_____

MARK McGWIRE: An easy-to-read photo-filled biography of one of baseball's
all-time greats. 32 pages, 8 x 8. $4.50 U.S.

_____

Total number of Book(s) Ordered   _____

Add $1.50 per book if you want book(s) autographed by author.   _____

Total Cost of Books   _____

TAX (NY State residents must add appropriate sales tax)   _____

Shipping Charges (in the U.S.) $2.50 per book, up to a maximum of $12.50
on orders of 10 or fewer books.
For international orders, email publisher for current terms.   _____

TOTAL PAYMENT ENCLOSED: (All payments must be in U.S. currency;
checks and money orders only; credit cards not accepted).   _____

(Please print clearly.)

NAME _____

ADDRESS _____

CITY_____ STATE _____ ZIP CODE_____

SEND PAYMENTS TO: **EAST END PUBLISHING, LTD.**
18 Harbor Beach Road, Miller Place, NY 11764

Discounts are available on orders of 25 or more books.
For details write or email: **rjbrenner1@gmail.com**

Terms are subject to change without notice.